Come the Harvest

Also by Paul Hunter

Ripening (2007)
Breaking Ground (2004)
Clown Car (2000)
Lay of the Land (1997)
Mockingbird (1981)
Pullman (1976)
Your House Is On Fire and Your
Children Are Gone (1970)

Come the Harvest

Paul Hunter

Silverfish Review Press
Eugene, Oregon

ACKNOWLEDGMENTS

Many thanks to the editors of the following publications, where some of these poems first appeared: *Prairie Schooner*: "Over the Deep Empty Answer" and "Dump." *Small Farmer's Journal*: "All of a Piece" and "You Ask Me." *The Southern Review*: "Between the Lines" and "In the Way of Things." *Spoon River Poetry Review*: "Afterlife" and "Pick."

"On the Rise" was offered as Wood Works pamphlet No. 80.

This publication was funded in part by a publishers fellowship from Literary Arts, Inc. in Portland, Oregon.

Published by
Silverfish Review Press
PO Box 3541
Eugene, OR 97403
www.silverfishreviewpress.com

Distributed by
Small Press Distribution
800-869-7533
orders@spdbooks.org
www.spdbooks.org

Library of Congress Cataloging-in-Publication Data

Hunter, Paul, 1943-
  Come the harvest : poems / by Paul Hunter. --1st ed.
     p. cm.
ISBN 978-1-878851-54-3
I. Title.
PS3558.U487C66 2008
811'.54--dc22

                                        2008004280

For Jerry, Judy, Mary, Gregory & Jennifer

& in memory of Christopher

who have loved the wilds
& the work of cultivation

with enduring thanks & love

Table of Contents

I. Whistling All the While

Over the Deep Empty Answer

Potty-trained in an outhouse when
without a sustaining grownup hand
the little one might simply jackknife in

one spring morning playing in the yard
alone maybe four I watched
two uncles tip up over on its ear
the little white box of nightmares
letting daylight into what I thought
an everlasting pit of stink that ran
black to the center of the earth

then one in hipboots staggered down
alongside the muck the other pointed out
was littered with flimsy love notes
and a delicate bite at a time shoveled it
up in the back of this wagon on iron wheels
while the horses stamped and studied
not spilling a drop onto anything
that they said they were stealing
to sweeten some feller's roses

then between us having heaped
this ripe understanding open-eyed
set the thing back good as new
right over the deep empty answer
harmless now as any lidded grave
then climbed to the seat took the reins
spoke once and the horses proceeded
down the road one said he heard
calling out some neighbor's mother load
whistling all the while the sunshine lasted

Like As Not

No matter what the young ones craved
in nightly prayers might blurt out
couldn't help themselves
squander the dime in their pocket
fling up a whole silver moon

begging parents for the bike
dollhouse radio electric train
roller skates mickey mouse watch bb gun
the response would come
as half a promise never more
once crops are in
once we know where we stand
we'll see come harvest time

so fall that bright red tractor first appeared
when the season was past needing one
when the money stood proud in our hand
fall was when the old folks took
that train trip way down south

came home with a nervous grin
some souvenirs they bought
a little something to show for
the parlor they didn't smoke in
that ashtray of the town of New Orleans
some chicory a fancy pair of spoons

worrying did they leave enough
to buy us Christmas presents

but mostly we'd make do
with hand-me-downs with
nothing much store-bought although
every three-four years might come
this wave of desire long denied
when we'd happen into some money
when the calves stayed healthy
the crop caught the rains just right
hit the market climbing not a drop

when all might approach the full table
share a little more than
was strictly good for them
that chocolate mint cream pie we bought
at a sitting polished off
with gingersnaps and orange pop
knowing full well by morning
everyone might suffer like as not

Country Girl

Squinting aproned freckled she
steps off the porch in hard sunlight
cotton dress for the heat
sewed herself for the fit
in high black rubber boots
rattling just below the knee
with the breakfast bucket of slops
peels shells and all set
to toss in the hog trough

she has already been out
reaching under hens to gather eggs
gauging their intermittent fuss
already helped throw together
the morning meal inhaled
half a minute then another
for the mop-up not a crust

now thinking ahead to her day
the stroll out to the mailbox
where from under her straw brim
the wind might worry free a lazy curl
the lotion she just rubbed
along both arms and legs
still slippery and cool

she is of an age that answers
most questions with a look
that her folks know can't help
craving every chance to run in town
to learn who she is or might be
not ready for the boys just yet

today waits her turn on the tractor
an afternoon plowing cornrows
satisfied she will be chosen since
she's steadier than her brothers
at the wheel more liable to follow
the planter's faint undulations
not tear up or bury with speed
these slight waving green apparitions
these lives that need to be left
like her cleansed their roots stirring
standing in the open undisturbed

Down to Earth

Dreamy kid until he started school
forced to turn out his pockets
tame a cowlick seemed to float along
a leaf on a quiet stream
drifting a world of its own

already discovered books
what else but craved to be
a kite aloft battling a breeze
all tattered bedsheet and lath
a pirate butterfly

growing straight up rickety
as a colt at daybreak unfed
that steals out barefoot overhears
sparrows clumped on a wire
debate a threatening cold snap

head full of scraps of ideas
but could already stand quiet
in line wait his turn always told
they still wished he would be
a little more down to earth

though what could that mean
to one who greets woken buds
feels tadpoles lip the bright surface
spots an eyetooth crack an eggshell
dawn swell its newly opened eye

On the Rise

Woven jammed under the bridge
that bears our business to town
the bridge it threatens to lift
float away on the rise
scour at erase the road itself
detour all commerce otherwise

find this nest spun so solid
stolen a scrap at a time
run off our fields swept together
scaffolds plumages love notes
figments mementoes and trash
loose change of the season just past

all winter laid still under blankets
stirred alive now as gifts of the thaw
resisting the flow and yet summoned
here to be interwoven
by chance first of the season
appearing so firm on its surface

of leavings discreetly confused
and roiling just under their snarl
at the season's early arrivals
as if sullen warning
none should choose here
to settle much less give birth

so in the end we climb aboard
this trembling momentary thing
that could let go any minute
and like fledgling lately orphaned birds
pick apart and one stick then another
send swirling down to the future

Volunteer

Sometimes up through compost
the first warm breath of spring
before they can be noticed
rooted out turned under

sunflowers will start poking up
squash leaf out notch by notch
ratchet all around take over
not exactly weeds reminders

of the strength of the season before
even once in a while a tomato
spindly thing will make a stand
pick the unlikeliest place to volunteer

presume in shade to flower
so determined a lesson in living
we leave well enough alone
maybe even grant a splash of water

Plenty More

With lemons hard to come by
but for trips to the city where
they might turn up in a market
and if so happens we're flush
snatched a good handful bought

to be halved by hand squozen
a few sliced thin nothing strained
stirred in the whole cup of sugar
taken in jars to the milk house
cooled for the trip to the field

to the ones in the hot sun haying
wet basketful under burlap
wait at the end of the row
shade for the team the break now
offered up handed around

to shake then unscrew the lid
sip cut the dust in the gullet
pucker chew lipsmacking laughing
then pour off the rest in one swallow
like there was always plenty more

Between the Lines

The new hired hand drifted
in with the harvest and stuck
not too old or too young
worked alongside the best of us
didn't smoke near the barn
had a wild lick of hair
big mouthful of teeth but
still kept his lip buttoned up

though when he'd come for his mail
I would notice him hang around
till there's no one else near
then step to the window
say his name softly and wait
with his hard open hand on the counter
made me think of
a mousetrap without bait

not that he got all that much
couple letters a month
and several times that first year
something looking official

this went on deep into fall
him out on one end of the porch
in shade fingers running
his hat brim around like
a wobbly straw steering wheel
eyes burning holes in it

till one day I hand him his mail
he points to the address
says what's that say
I say why that's your name
I know that part the B and W
but the rest there I tell him
that's how they find us
the route number name of
the town and so on
he looks around says
read it out to me would you mind

so I do though first I make
him tear it open himself
since mostly you try but can't help
seeing what's inside envelopes
which never mind illegal don't feel right

it's a letter from his ma
telling the news from back home
Carolina somewhere
about what you'd expect
crops and weather and weddings
no feelings to speak of
though looking off out the window
who knows what sinks in between the lines

when I'm done he reaches
in his hip pocket I think maybe
offering to pay but out comes
a wad of letters all the rest
tied up with string
postmarks right in order
opened studied folded put right back
every one of them for him a perfect blank

so I tell him come in Saturday
end of the day and we'll sit
read straight through the bundle

and when we do he learns
a girl he liked has had her second child
and back a year almost his father died

he asks if I'd help him write his ma
tell her how he's doing and the rest
though find some way to put it
that she'll think well of us
because it's not their fault
they kept me home at first
from scarlet fever I was sick
then started working the fields
seemed like they needed me
more than I needed myself

I go back behind the counter
dig out a nickel notebook pencil stub
that'll fit in the bib of his overalls
write two copies what he wants to say
hammering it out between us
the hardest kind of work there ever is

and make him keep the one
start lessons on it there and then
him printing out every letter
over the winter putting it together
till come planting time he can mostly
puzzle what he wants to say alone

Party Line

Because for years one busybody
Emma Hoffmeyer ran the switchboard
listened in on every little thing
and over Sunday dinner this

maiden aunt amused her family with
who did what where when
spilling the beans on
this whole end of the county

besides which one ailing neighbor
old Mrs. Metz nothing better to do
than count rings lift the earpiece
hold her ratchety breath

got so Mother and her married girls
would meet on the steps of the church
where menfolk pretend to politeness
really can't hardly wait breakfast

Sunday mornings name a time
later on to go pick up the phone
since we're all on the one party line
visit on family matters

even so in a country this quiet
you'd be met with knowing looks
sharp little comments
a nod of saintly forbearance

on your sister's rare female trouble
or how your brother's run off
got himself jailed in the city
practically everywhere you went

Lend a Hand

Never mind being safer
two heads better than one
we all know the work goes
smoother with another alongside
even small things like backing in
to hitch up big equipment
someone to yell whoa and drop the pin

still most of us these days
get by on our lonesome
since who can afford to share labor
fix a wornout hay bailer
that don't hardly pay worth beans

much less stand around hold the light for
the old man about to tackle
that burned-out starter motor
with the pickup hood sprung
spitting rain off and on
but start to hand the right tools
it now and again gets to be
kind of a minor symphony

one working up from down under
one reaching down from above
huffing clanging ratcheting
in time to the radio
caged droplight bulb a blink and sizzle

till the dirty old one falls away
gets a look and a kick to one side
to heft in place the shiny new one
feed the long bolts start the nuts on
take the weight of the thing
with scarce a whisker of clearance
wiggling that extra pair of hands
to get centered and seated
while the other tightens

then with one leaning back studying
what-all's come together
one eases in turns it over
starts with a roar and drives on

How Ripe

Two steps into these tasseled
green corn cathedral aisles
gold-dusted shoulders and elbows
that rustle and reach around as if
to usher a duchess in taffeta

you finger the heaviest ear
peel back shock silk and all
thumbnail a kernel to bursting
let juice spell how ripe for a sign
the crop will make the prayer end

then ahead to either side behind
sense crows not their wheeling
call to plunder from on high
much less bickering over crumbs
but settled eye-deep in the feast

polite amid plenty now plunge
in their sharp-bladed tongues
savor the sweetness the bounty
commence their dark chuckling over
who finally noticed who arrive

Spare the Horses

In a wagon heaped high as she'll go
and not tumble off in some ditch
you take to market every one you picked
no telling whatall they might fetch

only know you're going to need
every mouthful so want to drive slow
in your exhaustion at least recall
what to do to spare the horses

blowing hard climb each hill alongside
get down to walk then ride
the brake coming down the other side
to slow the load running over them

Weathered Wood

Some like to paint their barn a bible verse
some at the eaves a hex sign ward off evil
some paint all one color red or white
though some with time on their hands
run around the trim for the effect
they say helps keep up the rest
one painted in a scene of rolling hills
matching all those greens browns blues
as if to make his whole farm disappear

but then there are those
the Mail Pouch people got after
who even knowing they would paint
just the barn side facing the road
that the rest would be all up to you
that what you have up there to look at
sells everyone his uncle driving past
whether you chew or spit out
maybe the rest of your life
never will fade fast enough
not to show clean through a coat of black

which could be why some raise a barn
grow to like the look of weathered wood
that gets the more all the same
the longer you leave it alone

Dump

Though some old farms look to be perfect
off one corner somewhere still might be
a gully that naturally gathered
that rusty cookstove past repair
pickup that lit in a ditch
spewed its suspension all over
bedstead so squeaky who could stand
one more night of
wagon shed the rim off all its spokes
icebox the fieldmice dismantled
bicycle bent in a question mark
brokeback kitchen chair
every one of them going nowhere
but straight down into the ground
taking their own sweet time
where saplings creeper vines reach up
so better get out of the way
so no one gets hurt tripping over

except for the shop where you'd go
pull apart any thing still had life
most everybody used to feed a dump
you couldn't spot from the road
where secret failures were left
projects dropped once and for all
that rot and rust got the best of
hopes abandoned
all the breakdowns bad deals no deals
sure to be studied remembered
every time you boiled over went to throw
the latest costly lesson down that slope

Luminaries

If Charlie could get Evaleen
off her parents' porch swing
away from their yellow bug light
out in the cool night air
even along in their thirties
anything might still be possible

since she had already tried
the city boyfriend and job
neither quite working out
once more home for the summer
what might be his last chance

since childhood having known
each other both observe
the perfect decorum of those
who since first grade well aware
of the other's cosmic whereabouts
find themselves closer than words
though they've hardly actually spoken

so cultivating he thought
deep down the endless corn rows
for weeks enduring
a herkyjerk parade of sleepless nights
until at last in a fit he summoned up
what at the time she'd given scant regard
his high school science project

went straight to the pastor at church
asked permission to start
an astronomy club that won
the steely eye the blunt response for what
he said share the wonders of God

which is how the farmers came
Sunday night in the dark to stand around
his cardboard tube on its hind legs
in the gravel church parking lot

taking turns at the eyepiece
careful not to bump
as each leaving off tags the next
until all have gotten an eyeful
of the night's heavenly bodies

of which the celebrity dipped up
in his homemade ladle would appear
to be Saturn laid out on velvet
like a moth on the skin of a frog pond
quivering iridescent
trying not to flutter lest
something beyond make a meal of it

slight enough magic that yet
gives Evaleen reason to approach
ask after distant luminaries
brighter for the darkened countryside
her gardenia scent modestly intimate

as in reverend whispers they wonder
how Charlie could have ground by hand
a perfect saucer of this chunk of glass
adjusted until you could see
practically anything you'd care to look at
though nothing remains sharp for long
a few minutes and
it swims away out of their ken

still gives Charlie excuse
to hover about and refocus
offer cookies a thermos of coffee
though soon as one farmer commences
yawning till the others catch his drift
the gathering evaporates
till with no one else about
he spreads a blanket over dewy grass

where both sit stiffnecked lean back
still thankful for something to look at
as he points out the few he can recall
and she makes up names for a couple
as the night wheels on parade
their few points of meaning half-hid
by endless nameless scattered lights
where reaching through all that emptiness
their fluttering hands touch at last

Fair

Late summer crops done practically back to school
between county and state fairs still before
too much cotton candy on the tongue
over one long weekend all converge
for the town's own miniature fling

walk this plank and plywood arcade
where everyone craves to fit in
if only to wrap pennies pop balloons
play one others' ring-toss games
peddle baked goods lemonade
slather barbecue sauce stand entranced
by the taffy machine's loopy dance
climb the plump Shetland pony
led stiff-legged blindered
round its schoolyard ring
or in the church bingo tent
join old folks and kids
each playing three-four cards
plunking corn kernels down
all set to pounce eagle-eyed

or drawn to the two rented rides
one wobbles round an iron track
while the other wheels in the sky
that everyone has to try
for the drop in the pit of the stomach
the trembling rush of cool air
that practically stops your heartbeat
lets your life at this crossroads
make as if to catch its fevered breath

though come nightfall nothing outdazzles
the plain old kissing booth
church fathers can't quite approve
still know enough to wink at
that in daylight draws blushes
though after they auction box lunches
couples steal off then drift back
toward evening wearing
a brighter layer of lipstick

and though used to amusing ourselves
sometimes a stranger will appear
to wolf our pie sashay our pretty girls
family out for a drive or kids next town over
come join our own loners at loose ends
drawn straight to the dunking booth

where the prettiest girl or stout lad
gingerly takes up that trick seat
over the dark tank of water
where those known too well maybe
thinking themselves unloved
line up to plunk down
three potshots for a dollar
that after wild throws and near misses
the bullseye welcomes at last
with a clank of approval a splash

mister or miss popular
transformed this instant
to sputtering water rat
proving nobody is perfect
testing who stays a good sport

and for the fair's late unwinding
the ferris wheel at last fills
for a night view ravishing all around
while the machine going nowhere
trails screeches and sparks
hurdy gurdy tunes warbled
through blinking colored lights

spinning those held together
in one drowsy spell marveling
over this rolling farm country
newly shorn in the moonlight
amid jerks trembles catches
to open and shut the lap bar
as in a shambling dream unwound
one at a time is helped down
thankful to set foot on solid ground
while the rest hang suspended
patient in their slight eternity
feet treading summery air

II. What the Fence Caught

The Far Side

Maybe you grieve a lost love
worry that late loan come due
try on the new nightwatchman job
anyway burn up a night or two

and harrowing a field you might doze
slump at the controls and run
clean through the end of the row
snap three strands of barbed wire

gather it behind you in a snarl
scour across the county gravel road
nod into a ditch engine laboring
lean back strain upward wade

on into neighbors' winter wheat
where chugging along resting easy
hands loosen eyes dawn at last
still aimed for woods the far side

Pick

The local boys I tagged around behind
those days what with the war
the great depression both fought
grubbing in the dirt between
belt tightening and shell shock

had enough farming to last them
said the old ways were done
even with the GI Bill to fall back on
no craving to get them a place
slap up a house go to college
if you were single why bother
the ground planting anything

so into their thirties and forties
most sat around drinking beer
playing poker talking girls and cars
studied each hand for the omens
allowed they were looking to get on
road crew construction what have you
or best of all the distillery
a river town forty miles off
where to hear the boys tell it
every man-jack worked a pick

which like as not would amount
to a little medicine bottle
with a string round its neck
that hung from the top buttonhole
of your bib overalls
down inside the stovepipe legs

so you could stand by the vat
stirring sweeping drop your pick
let it fill slowly pull up
lower down your pantsleg
wander off to where
you could duck down take a nip

and round their penny ante game
these layabouts heard tell
only lucky ones never got caught
and how day shift and night shift
most worked drunk
and what a joy that must be
to never feel a blessed thing
at the whistle stagger out
already a load on
not a soul sniping at you
your whole day or night still ahead

Rural Delivery

One day walking home from town
with a brand-new fan belt round my neck
hot and smelly not a breath of air
like a dead rubber blacksnake self-evident

Lonnie slows for a rolling chat
offers a ride along his postal route
the car so full of his bundles
there's no place to sit but the driver's seat

with him not riding shotgun alongside
more a giant spider reaching round
to stuff the mail in boxes spin the wheel
lefthanded using what they call

a suicide knob lover's button take your pick
either way with his left foot
mash both gas and brake
jabbering away a mile a minute

swears he's first in these parts to go buy
an automatic let him get away
with all this wrongside driving
like a herkyjerk ichabod anyhow

basketball whiz till that knee quit
does things who else would even think to try
like here weaving down the road pull
a double u-turn fancy hiwaycop maneuver

grown man showing off for all he's worth
me thinking should that trick knee
lock up could I snatch
the wheel stomp my foot on his

in time to save us eating gravel
slid headlong into the inevitable
which might hurt his feelings so bad
he'd forget which mailbox is mine

lose whatever might have been
delivered to me till I'm ninety
so maybe best just let us run
off the road in the crick right here

find out who can dog paddle
else jump out the next row of boxes
thank him kindly slip on through bobwire
and beeline the rest of the way

Escape Artist

Edwin had one cow so smart
she could work any gate on the place
with a tongue as good as a hand
lift the catch slide the bar lip the chain
up over the post lean on slats
till it yawns wide or snaps

said he wouldn't mind
her taking a stroll if
only she'd close the gate after
but high noon or midnight
there they are strung out
along the road all together

so first thing he tries the obvious
but doesn't much care for
that big wad of keys
says it wears out your pockets
and gets lost in plain sight
just like your milk cows

so rather than change his old ways
and start toting a hacksaw
or risk breaking her heart
he trades her off to a neighbor
with greener pastures
who won't mind messing with locks

Banjo

Tommy's dog so tireless and quick
would play outfield for both teams
catch flies dive clean through the fence
fish homeruns out of the crick

so smart he wouldn't do tricks
play dead shake or fetch didn't bother
barking at strangers knew enough
not to worry porcupines and skunks

though in a fit of foolishness
he could be egged to take after a barn cat
he wouldn't kill or hunt
you'd go to shoot a bird

set to flush it lift your gun
he'd give you this look
run home dive under the porch
till the thunder was over and done

but how Banjo earned his keep
since practically a pup
was bring the cows in
every night himself

all it took was a whistle and point
here they'd come to be
shut in till daylight Tommy swore
he had ears like a bat else could count

because one time with one short
he dragged Tommy back to where
this heifer had her tail caught
in bobwire like to pulled it off

All of a Piece

Chestnut horse one day appears
pastured two miles up the road
with all those lush acres to graze
waits by the gate where he's left
every time you go by there he is

standing ears up skinny hopeless
waiting through every day for
someone to come for him though
how are they to know maybe never
once looked back over their shoulder

at this ordinary plain brown horse
not one spot of black or white
no star marker stocking point anywhere
mane and tail like the rest
well past the full bloom of youth

yet no touch of grey at the muzzle
no knock-knee swayback lean but sound
one whose beauty once all of a piece
was simply the life coursing though it
playful curious thoughtlessly alert

now nothing but a large dark steady eye
follows whoever drives by
so the whole summer in passing
we make up myriad reasons
excuses why he's abandoned

figure probably the neighbors' girl
college bound to break off a romance
or some gentleman farmer took sick
rodeo cowboy thrown hard broke his hip
maybe half his own fault aimed a kick

take a while to forgive and forget
though we all know most likely just another
worker out of a job who got dropped
by someone half expects he'll disappear
before they think to come back pick him up

Pet

His first year in 4-H Ben figures
the perfect place to start would be a pig
since they eat and get fat end of story
all you do for show is hose it off

so they let him pick one out
bring it home in his lap in the car
slap a shed of old boards together
decide where and when to feed and water

warn him not to play with it too much
and though it gets to be kind of a drag
those dark frosty mornings before
sunrise and the schoolbus he persists

even gets good at it somehow
the pig always lights up to see him
Ben figures because he means food
but with no other piglets about

who else is there to study and reflect
and with nose in the air snuffling
right away is named Snuffy
and well-fed grows up in a hurry

till one fine spring day Hanrahan
the 4-H advisor comes around
to check how his pig's getting on
one look and he says it's too fat

tells Ben put the pig on a diet
says most like em leaner and meaner
do whatever works to make him sweat
only don't turn him into a pet

which is twice as hard as it appears
with a no-neck beast big as he is
too smart to fetch a wornout tennis ball
even with a peanutbutter lick

much less do tricks for dog biscuits
so come feeding times he leads
Snuffy all over the pasture
rattling that bucket out ahead

once in a while sure to stumble
to let old Snuf hit the jackpot
though he mostly has to run to catch
his dinner a bite at a time

chase turned to kind of a dance
how much of a taste will inspire him
how much to hold back
till the worn-out pig loses interest

how much to finally let him have
and come time for the midsummer fair
when Ben goes to show off the pig
trails without a leash around the ring

on command stands and sits
and from some fancy restauranteur
at auction brings top dollar
that Ben is relieved to have done with

more than the slow motion pursuit
of an ideal pig physique
to end between friends this pretense
of who's training who and for what

Caught

After weeks being passed by ignored
stock-still by the gate to the pasture
why should she crave any
taste of the rust-roughened bit
embrace of cinches pulled tight
weight of the heartless fool on her
affection belied by neglect

so catching the pony to ride
once a cheerful seduction
now comes down to
a tug of war between
your guilt her resistance
your impatience to be done
with the feint rear and buck
the kick away behind
the ears-laid-back rush
past you in a smoldering stalk

a matter not of how long
will she remember but how long
will she hold it against you
that you both know sooner or later
could come to a bad end
a barbed wire tangle
slash one the other or both

so tail switching head turned
she ignores all entreaties soft words
pretends not to notice enticements
carrot or apple you've brought
which if you're smart you begin
eating so she can smell
figures she has to surrender
quick save a taste for herself

if you're lucky overlooks
the bridle undone behind your back
that now she has grown wary
the jingle and clink of it spooks

that in extremity you have to
abandon on a fencepost
as in widening circles she ranges
think to unloosen your belt
that when she comes close
to lip then munch at your offering
around her neck slip and buckle
that while she rears once
you hang on your full weight
till with a skitterish dance
she nods and settles
accepts once again she is caught

A Little Something for Everyone

We mow the fragrant clover and let lie
then rake in windrows
that all at once expose
townships of field mice and gophers
their myriad comings and goings
their living beneath what was planted
all their secret porches lookouts holes

soon for the easy pickings snakes converge
hoopsnakes copperheads kings
range the killing ground
who can blame them feasting
a month's worth in minutes
while overhead hawks
swoop and circle ravens owls

who without the bother of hunting
take their pick of this bounty
as unable to swallow even
one more furry morsel
in plain sight of the mayhem
snakes lie gorged
too drowsy too stiff to slither off

and as about to bale we rake again
take one more turn to let dry
in broad daylight a she-fox drags out
the last hidden pirate overstuffed
thrashes it back and forth
then home to the young in her den
canters waving her trophy

Snake Heaven

On the tractor Bill keeps a big wrench
never fit a thing he said was for
should he ever come across a poison snake

that he has nothing personally against
mostly copperheads no bother
provided you're watching your step

that might surprise young ones
tend to sleepwalk without
a rattler's fair warning to wake em

that on this hillside scrub pasture
like to hunt bird eggs and chipmunks
sun themselves all in among the rocks

a regular little snake heaven
where Bill figures keep an eye out
the right tool handy though I never see

him jump down make use of but once
then burying shake his head
like a case of mistaken identity

Vigilant

Without any children Bill kept
the scattergun behind the kitchen door
shells on the sill overhead
swollen beside the spare keys
where he'd look out over the yard
where in daylight under dappled
honey locust shade the hens ran free

and if in the night any ruckus
snatched him up out of sleep to where
he might spot the culprit reappear
with a mauled hen in its jaws
bloodless sadly shrunken
he might cut loose dust its backside
though mostly fair warning
blasting the still night air

and sometimes even broad daylight
might start from a nap in his chair
at the hawk's black shadow circling
or perched in a treetop
where he'd have to step off the porch
to wave and cuss it

he'd always notice which got caught
Delaware Rhode Island Red
Plymouth Rock Leghorn Barred Guinea
not which fattened up laid best
but which most needed minding

and the only ones he could flat out admire
were banties that like as not would roost
in a tree without a low limb
where their gaudy rooster kept lookout
that with daybreak fluttered down
to nest in weeds all around
where tiny eggs not worth the bother
proceed to hatch out underfoot to where
toward sundown he'd make as if
to shoo them in the coop
and watch them scatter

Shooting Rats

Usually there would be action
but if the dump was too quiet
we'd break open garbage bags
stir up something ripe

then sit in the dark listening
for them to get busy
then the one with the light
would take aim flip it on

pick the red eyes out
while the other one with
the .22 automatic would
do the job empty it

then we would trade so
the other at least got a turn
though again we'd sit quiet
reload settle into the nightlife

let them forget and go
back to whatever they did
nights which is not true some
would start eating others

just killed so the first
burst was always the best
which belonged to the one
who owned the Winchester

a couple rounds apiece and
they would be onto us
nothing left on earth had
a stink could draw them out

we got good enough we could
only go maybe once a month
otherwise let them calm down
dispose of their dead

relapse and raise a new crop
trusting and innocent
we never did call it rat hunting
we knew even then

the dump was like a village
where some simply lived
on what the rest would throw out
and that they were smart

though considered kind of
a lowlife set against us
treated with traps and poisons
which meant a fight to the finish

which may be why no one asked
where we went or said stop it
though anyone with ears
could tell what we were about

For a Good Time

With nothing to do of an evening
the day's one train come and gone
we would drive to a grade crossing
swing around line up onto the tracks

let a little air out of the tires
turn up the carburetor idle screw
then put the car in gear
and when we were going along

smooth at an easy lope
nicely following the rails
no feet no hands no eyes
climb out the windows up onto the roof

and ride along drinking beer
through this empty farm country
waving and nodding like we were
on parade some crazy lost caboose

Night Train

You could always tell
in the scheme of things
just where you stood
wrong place the right time
what's not looking to collide

out on the farm even
miles from nowhere
every night the same time
to the minute you'd hear
the train whistle

for that grade crossing
one long moan through
the heart of your town
hellbent stone-blind
wide open throttle

Gazebo

On the farm turned over to the kids
who now mostly do the heavy lifting
work their own ideas
where the old folks lend a hand
with haying canning
help the numbers come out even
hardly a thing on the place in their name
any more but the riding lawnmower

still by the lake dug for watering livestock
now fenced out the kids poured
a concrete pad over which they threw up
what they like to call the gazebo
in time for that golden anniversary
who cares it's not much to look at
really just a pole barn frame
holds up a square metal roof
stops rain throws a decent patch of shade

that they plan to screen in
should the bugs get really bad
but for now hate to block the view
well away from the house
four sides open all directions
airing the faintest impressions

where in season they put out
some comfortable chairs
might get a little damp who cares
mom and pop recliners matching pair
bug torches barbecue grill
cooler full of refreshments picnic table
everything you'd care to play
horseshoes badminton croquet
whatever you might want except TV

so of an evening here they set
watch the grandkids fish off the dock
close enough to blow a nose or bait a hook
straighten out a birdsnest spinning reel
help chase a toad or garter snake
punch holes in a jar lid
to go gather lightning bugs
or see if they can maybe interest
one or another pulling grass
poke through the fence to feed some cows

sensing this may be the one
summer of the kind they'll likely get

every night hold off late as they dare
lighting bug torches
loving how the light lingers
little ones climb into laps for the show
settling last on the mirror
dimpled by a million feeding fish
where herons stalk the shallows
bats do their broken aerobatics
and providing they're all good and quiet
deer drawn down the hillside
clear the fence without a thought to steal a drink

III. Long Way Home

All There Ever Was

I

Though in time there came to be
a station to pump gas and patch a tire
there was no grain elevator no feed store
no barber shop or tractor parts
no savings and loan no police
no town hall mayor justice of the peace
no dancehall roadhouse no antiques
no coffee shop no parking lot
and though nearby tracks ran past
not even a whistle stop

what there was and is
maybe a dozen families huddled close
another fifty farming the periphery
around a crossroads with a dogleg
by the church and school
sure thing for a team and wagon
a hard right then a hard left either way
hard on those horseless contraptions
once or twice a year would land a car
smack in the ditch or the garden

right where from early on grew up
a post office general store
out back a wagon maker
nearby lunchcounter saloon
the other end of town the undertaker

what more did they need
some played organ others sang the choir
some worked at keeping up the roads
fixed what broke down cut each other's hair
tended the sick best they could
traded what they lacked or went without
borrowed and loaned out the rest
there was no government to speak of
not much call for law and order
when someone was fit to be tied
until he slept it off
their rope was good as a jailer

what the county labeled unincorporated
dot on the map with no name
what folks passing through
never slowed to admire
might call a wide spot in the road
that if you didn't know
where to look you'd never find
that's been right here forever
like a quiet old tune we remember
everyone humming along

2

Never mind the Depression gushed
all that red ink on the books
after the war the store dwindled
faltered when they pushed through
the interstate a dozen miles away
close enough that anyone could take
their new car on a whim
clean to the city to spend
that GI money seeing sights and once
you've learned your way around

the supermarket aisles took in
the odd out-of-season produce
all those fancy pickle jars

what good is a general store
with just the basics
a little baked goods dry goods
yard goods and hardware
baskets of what everybody grows
with one handcrank gas pump
the glass counter frosted
from all the nickels slid across
for red and black licorice whips
jawbreakers horehound drops

so first there's no more bread because
it goes hard as a rock in the case
then crumbling cookies and crackers
till after a while even glue and paint get old
colors fade the ends of bolts of cloth
since who has time nowdays for sewing
and there you are taken to dusting
canned goods coal oil lanterns
shining dollar pocket watches
oiling brand-new Barlow knives
that like to rust sitting there
where you once sold a dozen a year

3

Still who can't summon the sound
of the bell nailed over the front door
tinkle twice opening closing
or summer screen door yawn and slap

how folks would roam the aisles
linger over every notion to admire
like it hadn't sat right there for years
its handlettered tag in plain sight

though in season the drummer might
drop off a little something cause a stir
lavender soap harness buckles
latest cotton print with tiny flowers

4

But then in their wisdom all the powers that be
turned State Route One into a trucking route
went to the old man lived behind
the empty husk of a store
who in his youth also taught
what passed for school in these parts

offered to pick up and move the whole shebang
buy him out or cut in half
to widen their right of way
take out that dogleg
straighten and smooth out the trouble

he said cut it in half so they did
cut the wide shaded porch the store entry
that looked out over the cemetery
where beside his wife his place was set
then sided over what was left
and there he sat rocking his memories
all turned to face the wrong way

so now the rigs at fifty barrel through
trembling the single-paned glass
never let up on the hammer
or if they do slow for a look
around this drowsy hamlet
right at the ghost of the dogleg
treat townsfolk to the jake brake's rattatat

5

And with no store at all now
kids bused the next township over
mail delivered far and wide what's left
to pull together all there ever was
to meet a body's needs
here make a place that would stick

but a little visit Sundays
down the front steps after church
the rare wedding christening funeral
maybe potluck bingo twice a month
where folks bring a hot dish
linger to swap stories recipes
where like as not you will hear
a few still make do the old ways
while most drive the long miles to work
call farming a hobby for weekends
garden and can out of habit
a little on the side just chicken feed

say with that old backwards humor
they'd just as soon quit all this
grubbing in the gound
but come spring there you are
like you woke up with a pitchfork
someone put glue on the handle
you can't seem to turn loose of
with all these chores to get done

What You Found

What turned up dull behind the plow
caught the eye reined in the team anyhow
called for the stumble down reach
to scrub on pantsleg or sleeve

then wrap in a tired handkerchief
shine the pocket all day up and down
till inside come sundown to rest
surprise one and all what you found

study squinting pass from hand to hand
speculate whatall must have been
somehow dropped on your land
tucked in folded dirtbound overlooked

that Saturday can't wait to run to town
to pass round the little store offer
the schoolmaster pile in his shoebox
with others that fell from the sky

rose in thaw from a burial once from the vast
inland ocean long since washed ashore
to show children come Monday morning
what appears to belong to us all

Ordering the Stone

Looking after all those gone before
even babes in arms best they could
folks nearly always found a way
to put up a decent headstone

sometimes having to wait
for that one year in seven
for it to all come together
weather markets every growing thing

and since Sundays they'd wander
the graveyard and study
what time rains the lichen
did to even the strongest

simplest names and expressions
of love everlasting
ordering the stone they would tell
the man cut it deep make it shine

The One Thought

Even after something like success
once he'd accepted all a team could do
not work themselves to death

how with shelter and maintenance
any manmade thing could outlast him
how to take decades balancing the books

still he wouldn't mess with flowers
left picking posies to the womenfolk
until practically the last year of her life

took beauty straight from the field
he said packed into one dense crop
all its vigor uplift and profit

till with her bedrid and restless
all at once he starts to pitch in more
than occasional wheelbarrows of manure

all round the house weeds and waters
becomes almost a flower connoisseur
and as the point sinks in then buys

himself a box of honeybees to work
blossoms with bonnet and smoker
and through her last winter finds out

like a stalled team he always has to feed
never overcrowd or overlook
else the first warm windless day

a furry golden ball might issue forth
like a great mind with the one thought
to leave him and never come back

The Other Thought

Fifty years in the fields
he could no more busy
himself around me
the whole day than pigs fly

still he did come inside
do what must have been
all along in his nature
cook wash dishes unasked

as for tending flowers that
beekeeping rig he put on like
an old lady needing to keep
herself out of the sun

I told him kindness
seems a poor disguise
for the thief of honey
seeing them swarm over him

like a shimmering planet
a fur coat almost like love
told him how heartless
in the fall they'd come to be

how the workers sting
the male drones out of doors
to make less mouths
to winter over

watched him go study
then come in set on the bed
to tell how they poured out
dead on the stoop like I said

What Goes

No telling how much use any man
might make of his father's hay wagon
from century before last
but for all the years it's good to know
what keeps up with changes what lingers
what falls away what permanently goes

so first to drop aside the wooden axles
which happened the year or two after
the team passed on when the tongue
was cut singletrees scrapped a clevis
welded to fit tractor bar drop pin

then over the next dozen years
iron-rimmed wood-spoke wheels
got swapped for steel all around
Chevrolet rims rubber tires
that starting off over gravel
lost that crunch the first footfall
that musical ringing clatter on a roll

till finally the stepped plank bed
with its high wooden forks either end
perfect holding loose hay billows swirls
was unbolted heaved away to be replaced
by a level bed to stack rectangular bales

till by now all that's left
are the two long conestoga timbers
old growth elm curved end to end
laddered inletted crossbraced
double spine that you can only see
providing you drop to one knee
for a look what holds together
down from above upward from below
this essence of structure in motion
tucked under where it never even shows

Corn Jabber

To work what he calls the corn jabber
you hold the wood handles apart
stick the iron-tipped duckbill

into loose dirt then push
the handles together which
opens up a little slit

at the same time from
the hopper fed by its little
ratcheting wheel underneath

down will drop a kernel
landing just about right
after which you pull apart

and lift the whole thing up
does practically everything but
kick dirt in the hole to finish it

their oldest simplest planter
from century before last this
is what you still use wherever

ground moles get after the seed corn
hoping to save yourself a little
bending down fingering

each new life in the dirt
no matter how big the field
worked double-tired four-wheel drive

diesel everything still you climb
down to plant on foot by hand
wherever nothing comes up

Promise

Once we'd save our own seed corn
pick the brightest best ears
from the crib for next year
by girth taste and color

shuck by hand store
in ratproof steel milk cans
cool dry cache with a promise
all we had this year and more

but now every spring we go buy
hybrid seed packed in plastic
sterile glazed with insecticide
that in the final extremity

you couldn't eat if you had to
no matter the bag's pretty picture
what you get you hope you never see
corn with no past and no future

Holdout

On a trampled scrapend of pasture
what's left of the last farm in town
shrinks down into itself

barn finally painted just so
loud handful of chickens let go
fence all around set to sing

road frontage sold off for taxes
though behind every back yard
reminders what all this used to be

surrounded cut off by the rest of us
built up shoulder to shoulder
each sculpted grander than the last

still going to and fro we see
in overalls and straw hat the holdout
fork manure on his vegetable patch

and out from under a shade tree
down what used to be its own hillside
in its own good time staggers

the lone swayback horse
now unworked underfed that still
keeps this green hole from closing

by standing resting one fetlock
by simply lowering
his long head to graze what is left

You Ask Me

The old farmer taking
a walk through what used to be
his fields smack in the center
of a brand-new development
says most of us can't bear
to look back over our shoulder

though after all this is
the one crop still makes money
same time makes no sense
we're not running out of
mouths to feed any time soon
and should live closer together

but you ask me they'll have to
dig all this back up to plant
something healthy providing
they've still got sun and rain
a supply of seed and remember
where it all grew once upon a time

Serious

He runs a strand of electric fencing
four inches high round his garden
then another twenty inches or so

with no gate no breaks anywhere
easy for a man to clear
providing he watches his step

the low one makes the most trouble
since he has to keep mowing
so weeds don't start to short out

his setup is tailored for raccoons
too smart for ordinary fence
that play hell with certain crops

crookneck squash butter beans
though his asparagus
they leave pretty much alone

if this was the farm's furthest corner
he might have deer to worry
which can prove irresistible

even so he has had a mother coon
lead her young in set up camp
in the corn patch until it was gone

any more he doesn't hold with guns
so pelts with rocks till they move on
though as he still likes to say

he is serious about his sweet corn
which when it comes in is like heaven
nowhere does it say you have to share

Where Hope Springs

Though these parts they farm the old way
rainwater stays put where it's fallen
plant with a lick and a promise
worry high clouds what is coming
count your blessings one year out of three

down off that rise where the house sits
where his grandfather and father elected
to build rebuild add onto all around
right where someone of his name
chooses to live to this moment

below the barn in the pasture
Edwin one day deep in
the worst of the Depression found
a soft swampy spot where
water seeps out of the ground

dug in there for the catchment
formed up and poured the cement
framed in and lidded a pumphouse
commenced to watering livestock
seventy-five years and more

no matter what else became of
the herd the crops every dry spell
run clean through like a cloudburst
spilling sweet water aplenty
hope never once has run dry

Crossfire

Over new-mown hay with
scarce a hitch or collision
shuttle barn swallows

the wheel and swoop of their hunt
their darting dance
one with the harvest

where in mid-flight
over fluttering morsels
child parent sibling and lover

crossfire sharp cries of pleasure
where through loops and swirls
screeling uplifts and scrolls

drawn in discreet parallel
two cleave together
brush tapered wingtips and part

weaving invisible
threads in the sunset
stitching up workers and whatnot

till cooling air dampens
day's final insect
and as night tunes its chorus

and the first bat staggers
onstage its bold imitation
rickety random erratic

alongside and out ahead
bound home under rafters
all race the gathering dark

Afterlife

Sown in their jostling millions
growing all the same height
till greengold the plains undulate

in unison sunflowers track
dawn to dark their namesake
through the night swing around

so upturned they wait
as if outside kindergarden
facing the door of first light

which goes on each head swiveling
east to west through the south
at dark ratchets back a slow dance

beloved of redwing blackbirds
who splash about sunset colors
upend their calls liquid crystal

all summer long till at last
swollen blackened faces tucked
out of west winds come to rest

each still facing the footsteps
and crack of the coming dawn
with nothing more to learn

from a gaptoothed afterlife
spilling dry tears from the battered
blind satchel it's become

Leaning on the Top Rail

How can one person's heaven
be any other's unless
heaven is anywhere
peace and plenty
happen to come together

like these heifers turned out
into new pasture
so deep it tickles their bellies
that you can see from
their tails as they graze
in and out of each other
all switching lightly

that dance of approval
better than a grin
that dawns in unison
on some kindergardeners
that will be heaven until
they all get a bellyful
or something new comes along

and leaning on the top rail
I don't like to think
what hell for them must be
my teacher in school said
Dante the poet would tailor
a different one for each sinner
no two punishments alike

nor do I like to think
what hell might turn out to be
for the likes of folks who make
these calves end bunched in terror
bawl as a hand plucks them out
takes them down quick one by one
in no particular order

What You Never Touch

Though at first what you care for
finger into the ground feed and water
in the end gather up and carry off
that draws your fullest attention

so your fields in season come to be
every spare moment what you
dream of where you roam at large
even at rest cultivate
shiver out of bed return to see
around the edges worry even so

toward the end of making up a life
of small lives in their myriads
every now and then will reappear
clippings and leavings let be
brambles a mind of their own
stones from the field down a gulley
brush without a thought accumulate

corner of woodlot let go
not a single useful sapling flung
up in the narrow sunlight
worthless impenetrable thicket

till at last you find practically
all you ever crave
is what you never touch
leave well enough alone to tend itself
the end of each field and fencerow
among weeds you never troubled
these faint rustling presences
come late gone early who knows
perfectly at home without you

In the Way of Things

Wind stirs what's left of the leaves
in the poplar stubborn hangers-on
some lift some twist and
bow to what moves them
not a one green
shades of gold and brown

they have already held on
through a couple storms
some may make it to Christmas
New Years tattered blackened
though come spring not a one
will be here in the way of things

the whole tree comes alive in a gust
settles for the moment then
high up in belated departure
one chooses or is chosen
volunteers or submits
lets go or is let go and drops

rocking its way down
through the still dark rising to meet it
like a tiny boat put to sea
open blind rudderless
lightly settling into the everything
billowing kin on the ground

More

Until the instant it goes
out of you with a sigh
there is always more to come
more than you realize
rattling down backroads

headed to work or resting
leaned on a fence rail
eyeing the weather more
cycled through every second
more simply hanging around

then out of shadows
one evening it dawns like
the shimmering edge of
this green spinning world
what you have been after

this life that for the moment
went along with you rarely
a rhythm breathed out and in
more like something you
desperate for nourishment

breathed in and swallowed
ignored while living on
finally treated like
something to spit out
some odd infection we share

that through these others
nearby will go on
as if you had never been
one with the world
one in a rare atmosphere

What You Did

Old folks would shake their heads say who you are
is not just where you went so you could talk
saw in some picture show studied up in some book
not what you bought to play with like a toy
not even what you saved or wished or dreamt

but what you did in the field in the open
with your own two hands and whatever
you could bring to hitch to the business
that might grow to stand on its own
let you rest in its shade and be quiet

Author's Note

Those old folks invested in me. Spilled the beans best they could, for such taciturn souls. When I would prod one-on-one they didn't hold back, didn't spare my feelings or their own much. The essence of poetry, couched in tangibles, offering life more cleanly felt in fewer words. And working alongside where sometimes I might as well have been invisible, I learned there were times to keep my questions and thoughts to myself, simply wonder and watch what turns up. What is the sky telling them it won't tell me? What are we likely harvesting today? And learned maybe to accept the precise mysteries of their doings, strung out beyond anything they'd say.

This book was set in Adobe Jenson, a faithful electronic version of the 1470 roman face of Nicolas Jenson. Jenson was a Frenchman employed as the mintmaster at Tours. Legend has it that he was sent to Mainz in 1458 by Charles VII to learn the new art of printing in the shop of Gutenberg, and import it to France. But he never returned, appearing in Venice in 1468; there his first roman types appeared, in his 1470 edition of Eusebius. He moved to Rome at the invitation of Pope Sixtus IV, where he died in 1480.

Type historian Daniel Berkeley Updike praises the Jenson Roman for "its readability, its mellowness of form, and the evenness of color in mass." Updike concludes, "Jenson's roman types have been the accepted models for roman letters ever since he made them, and, repeatedly copied in our own day, have never been equalled."

Silverfish Review Press is committed to preserving ancient forests and natural resources. We elected to print *Come the Harvest* on 50% post consumer recycled paper, processed chlorine free. As a result, for this printing, we have saved: 1 tree (40' tall and 6-8" diameter), 385 gallons of water, 155 kilowatt hours of electricity, 42 pounds of solid waste, and 83 pounds of greenhouse gases. Thomson-Shore, Inc. is a member of Green Press Initiative, a nonprofit program dedicated to supporting authors, publishers, and suppliers in their efforts to reduce their use of fiber obtained from endangered forests. For more information, visit www.greenpressinitiative.org.

Cover design by Valerie Brewster, Scribe Typography.
Text design by Rodger Moody and Connie Kudura, ProtoType Graphics.
Printed on acid-free papers and bound by Thomson-Shore, Inc.